Michael Jackson

SADDLEBACK
EDUCATIONAL PUBLISHING

Saddleback's Graphic Biographies

SADDLEBACK
EDUCATIONAL PUBLISHING
www.sdlback.com

ISBN-13: 978-1-61651-265-1
ISBN-10: 1-61651-265-2
eBook: 978-1-60291-945-7

Printed in Guangzhou, China
1110/11-09-10

16 15 14 13 12   1 2 3 4 5

Michael Jackson, the King of Pop, was the most successful entertainer of all time. He won 13 Grammy Awards and 26 American Music Awards. He had 13 *Billboard* "Hot 100" number-one singles.

Michael Joseph Jackson was born in Gary, Indiana, on August 29, 1958.

He was the eighth of 10 children. His father, Joe, was a steelworker. His mother, Katherine, managed the household.

Michael had three sisters: Rebbie, La Toya, and Janet.

Janet, let's put on your coat.

Michael also had six brothers: Jackie, Tito, Jermaine, Marlon, Brandon (who died before Michael was born), and Randy.

Michael, hurry! We're late for school.

Joe Jackson loved music. He played guitar in a band called the Falcons. But he couldn't support his large family playing music.

Take it again from the top.

When Michael was five, Joe created the singing group the Jackson Brothers. The group included Jackie, Tito, Jermaine, Marlon, and Michael. Michael played the tambourine and drums.

Practice makes perfect!

Joe was very strict. He made his boys play over and over again after school.

Michael, you're off the beat!

Ooh, I bet you're wondering how I knew About you're plans to make me blue...

In 1966 both Michael and Jermaine sang lead vocals. The group became known as the Jackson 5. They signed a recording contract with Steeltown Records in 1967.

It's a deal.

Barry Gordy, of Motown Records, saw the Jackson's audition tape.

Who are those boys?

In 1968 the brothers signed with Motown Records. Michael became the lead singer.

I am proud to introduce the Jackson 5.

Their first album, *Diana Ross Presents the Jackson 5,* was an instant hit. "I Want You Back" went to number one.

We have a number-one hit!

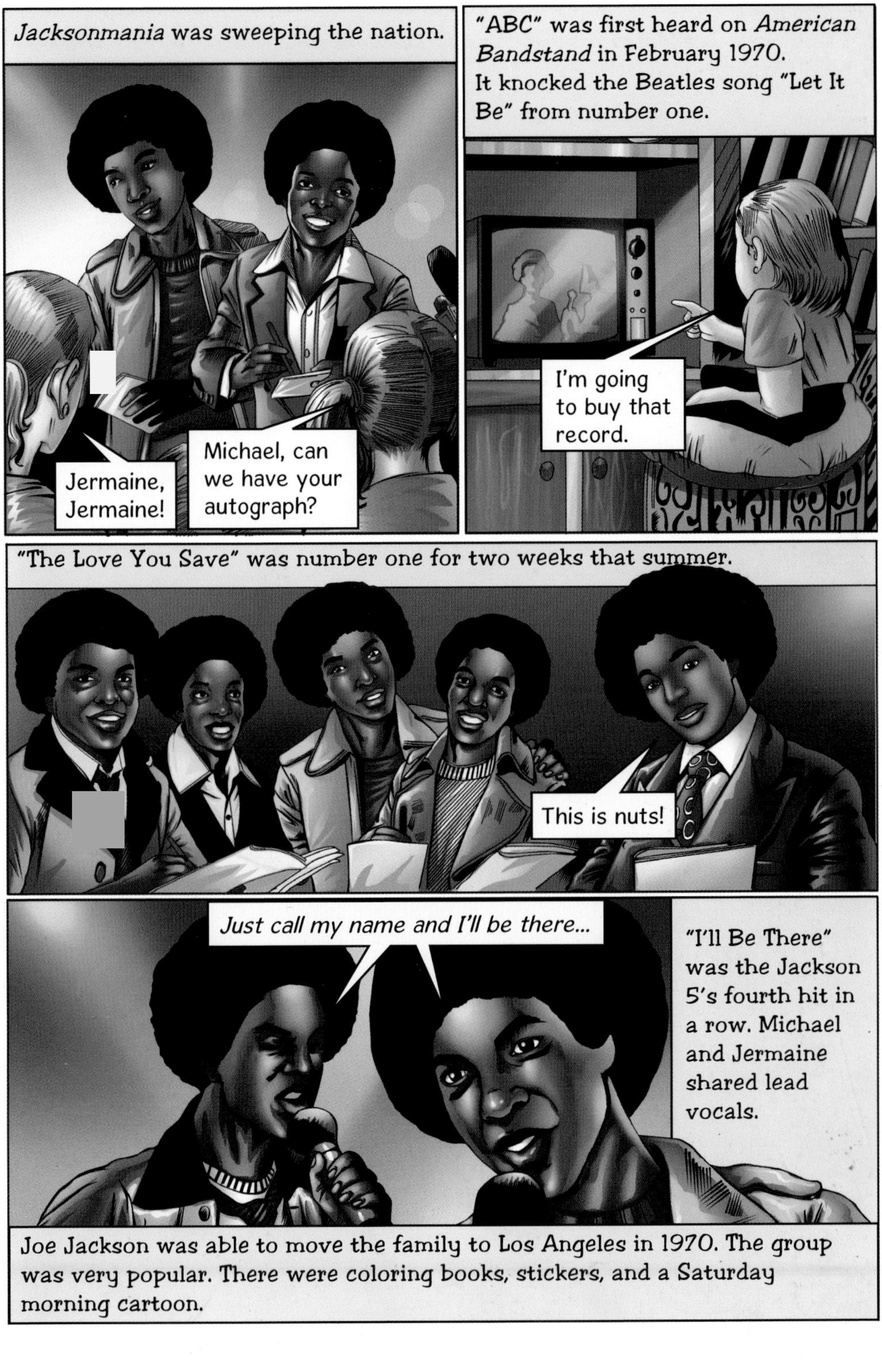
Jacksonmania was sweeping the nation.
Jermaine, Jermaine!
Michael, can we have your autograph?
"ABC" was first heard on *American Bandstand* in February 1970. It knocked the Beatles song "Let It Be" from number one.
I'm going to buy that record.
"The Love You Save" was number one for two weeks that summer.
This is nuts!
Just call my name and I'll be there...
"I'll Be There" was the Jackson 5's fourth hit in a row. Michael and Jermaine shared lead vocals.
Joe Jackson was able to move the family to Los Angeles in 1970. The group was very popular. There were coloring books, stickers, and a Saturday morning cartoon.

Motown knew that they had a star in Michael. In 1971 he released his first solo single "Got to Be There." His solo album sold over 5 million copies.

Let's get him back in the recording studio, pronto!

The single "Ben" from Michael's second solo album was nominated for an Academy Award. It won a Golden Globe.

And the winner for best song is...

And here's Michael Jackson singing "Ben."

Michael and Jermaine had solo careers. But the brothers continued to record together. After 1972, the group's albums were not as successful.

Marlon   Tito   Jackie   Jermaine   Michael

Joe Jackson was convinced that Motown was doing a bad job. He began to look for a new record company. In 1975 the Jackson 5 became the Jacksons. They signed with Epic Records, which was owned by CBS.

To promote the Jacksons, CBS signed the entire family to star in a variety show. The show would compete with ABC's *Donny & Marie.* It ran for almost a year and included Michael, Marlon, Tito, Jackie, Randy, Rebbie, La Toya, and Janet.

Michael became the lead songwriter for the Jacksons. He wrote "Shake Your Body (Down to the Ground)," "This Place Hotel," and "Can You Feel It."

Jackson starred in the movie musical *The Wiz* as the Scarecrow. Quincy Jones arranged the movie's score. But it flopped at the box office.

Mmm, whoa, la-la...

This movie stinks.

Michael teamed up with Quincy Jones who produced *Off the Wall.* When he finished recording, he fired his father as his manager.

Off the Wall was a huge hit. Michael won a *Grammy* Award. The single "Don't Stop 'til You Get Enough" went platinum (over 1 million sold).

Keep on with the force don't stop Don't stop 'til you get enough...

Just before Christmas in 1982, *Thriller* was released. Seven of the album's songs reached the top 10.

Thriller sold 110 million copies worldwide. It won a record-breaking eight Grammy Awards.

Thank you all.

Jackson turned the music video into art with special effects, famous celebrities, and complex dancing.

It's close to midnight and something evil's lurking in the dark
Under the moonlight, you see a sight that almost stops your heart...

With the release of *Thriller*, Michael became the most popular African-American artist ever. He met President Ronald Reagan at the White House.

The *New York Times* wrote that "in the world of pop music, there is Michael Jackson and there is everybody else."

In 1983 the Jackson 5 reunited in a TV special to celebrate Motown's 25 years. They sang some of their greatest hits. Then, Michael sang "Billie Jean." He performed the "Moonwalk" dance move for the first time.

And mother always told me be careful of who you love...

MICHAEL

For the first time, Michael wore one rhinestone-covered glove. It became his signature look. His performance brought down the house.

During the filming of a Pepsi commercial in 1984, Michael's hair caught on fire. He suffered bad burns on his scalp. To hide the scars, Michael had plastic surgery. And it wasn't the first time.

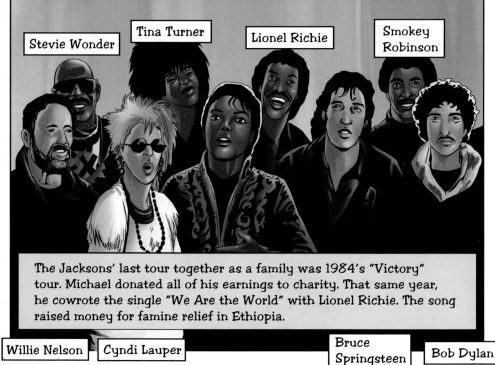

Stevie Wonder

Tina Turner

Lionel Richie

Smokey Robinson

The Jacksons' last tour together as a family was 1984's "Victory" tour. Michael donated all of his earnings to charity. That same year, he cowrote the single "We Are the World" with Lionel Richie. The song raised money for famine relief in Ethiopia.

Willie Nelson

Cyndi Lauper

Bruce Springsteen

Bob Dylan

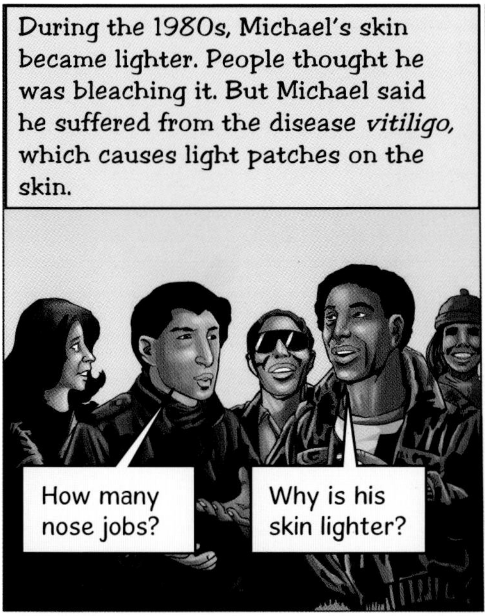
During the 1980s, Michael's skin became lighter. People thought he was bleaching it. But Michael said he suffered from the disease *vitiligo,* which causes light patches on the skin.
How many nose jobs?
Why is his skin lighter?

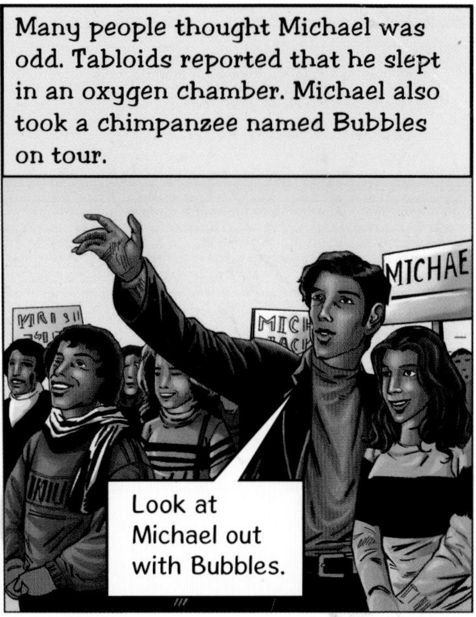
Many people thought Michael was odd. Tabloids reported that he slept in an oxygen chamber. Michael also took a chimpanzee named Bubbles on tour.
Look at Michael out with Bubbles.

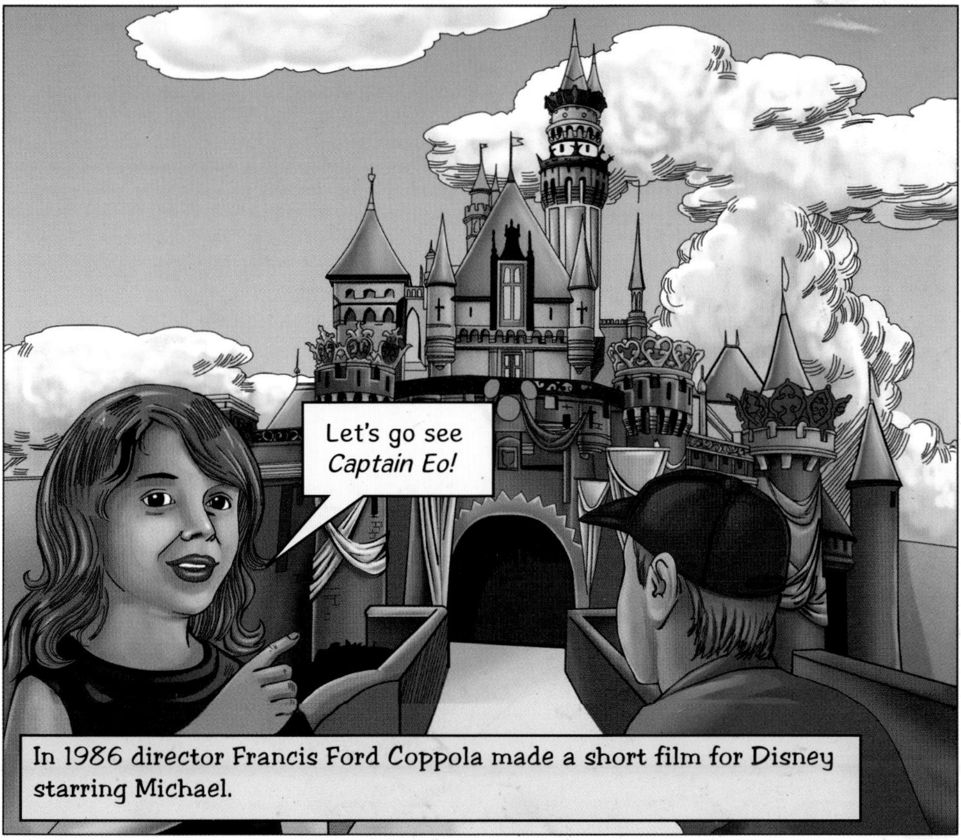
Let's go see *Captain Eo!*
In 1986 director Francis Ford Coppola made a short film for Disney starring Michael.

In 1987 Michael released the album *Bad*. Five singles from *Bad* hit number one.

During his tour, Michael released his autobiography. The book, *Moonwalk*, was edited by Jacqueline Kennedy Onassis.

Wow, this place is great!

During this time, Michael purchased Neverland Ranch in California. It had an amusement park, zoo, and movie theater. Michael had many overnight guests.

Michael had a lot of famous friends. He was close with Elizabeth Taylor, Macaulay Culkin, and Brooke Shields. Culkin stayed at Neverland Ranch many times.

Michael's eighth album, *Dangerous*, was released in 1991. Sony paid him $100 million to renew his contract. "Black or White" was the biggest hit on the album.

Congratulations, Michael.

It don't matter if you're Black or white...

The tour is over. I need to get home.

Michael ended the "Dangerous" tour early. He was accused of child molestation in the late summer of 1993. He took painkillers to deal with the stress.

Neverland Ranch was searched by the police. They were looking for evidence. Michael declared his innocence and cooperated with the investigation.

We have a search warrant.

His friends and family defended him. But Michael never recovered from the shame. Michael's insurance company paid a settlement. The case was dropped.

I know Michael is innocent.

Michael leaned on his longtime friendship with Lisa Marie Presley. She was afraid for his health.

Michael, you need to get some help.

Michael and Lisa Marie were secretly married in the Domi Republic on May 26, 1994.

"You Are Not Alone" from the album *HIStory*, debuted at number one on *Billboard's* "Hot 100" in August 1995. It was Jackson's last number-one song in the United States.

Another day has gone I'm still all alone...

News of Michael's marriage to Lisa Marie stunned the world. She appeared in his music video "You Are Not Alone."

That was Michael Jackson with another hit.

It's an honor to work with Michael. He is a perfectionist.

It's a good deal for me.

The *HIStory* album was nominated for five Grammy awards. The two-disc album contained older songs. New recordings included a duet with his sister Janet.

Michael was also making money as a businessman. He sold half of his interest in ATV Music Publishing to Sony for $90 million.

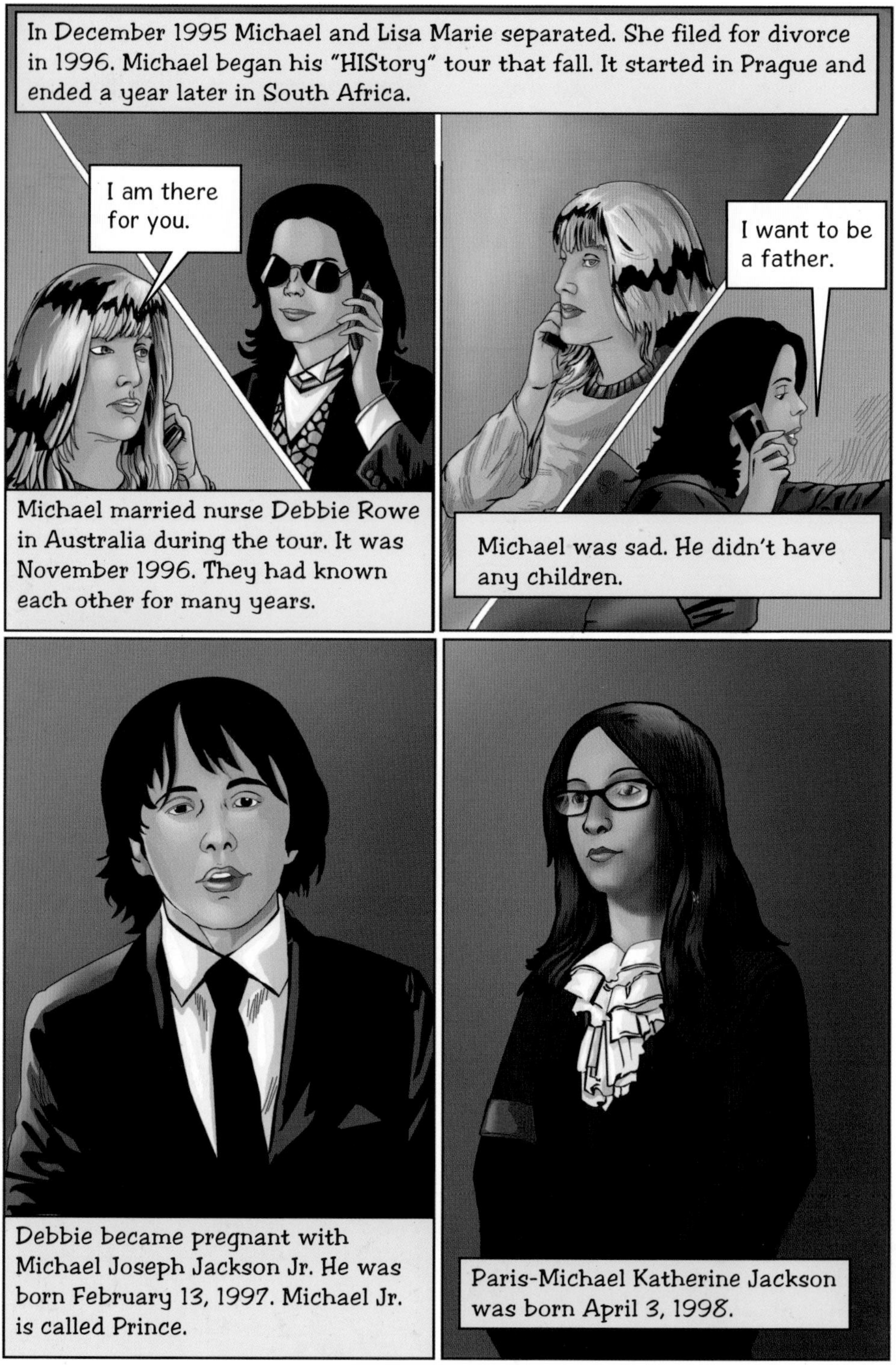
In December 1995 Michael and Lisa Marie separated. She filed for divorce in 1996. Michael began his "HIStory" tour that fall. It started in Prague and ended a year later in South Africa.
I am there for you.
Michael married nurse Debbie Rowe in Australia during the tour. It was November 1996. They had known each other for many years.
I want to be a father.
Michael was sad. He didn't have any children.
Debbie became pregnant with Michael Joseph Jackson Jr. He was born February 13, 1997. Michael Jr. is called Prince.
Paris-Michael Katherine Jackson was born April 3, 1998.

On October 8, 1999, Michael and Debbie divorced. Debbie gave Michael full custody of the two children.

Chris Tucker

Britney Spears

Whitney Houston

Usher

I am honored.

Destiny's Child

Over two nights in early September 2001, Michael performed at Madison Square Garden in New York City. Many stars honored Michael's 30 years as a solo artist. The Jackson brothers were reunited on stage for the first time since 1984.

Pink

Mariah Carey

Steven Tyler

Goo Goo Dolls

That October, after September 11, Michael organized a benefit concert at RFK Stadium in Washington, D.C.

Also in October 2001, Michael released his last album of new songs. *Invincible* was also Michael's last album released by Sony. *Invincible* went double platinum (selling 2 million units).

MICHAEL JACKSON
INVINCIBLE

Michael's third and last child, Prince Michael Jackson II, nicknamed "Blanket," was born in 2002. Blanket's mother is unknown.

From May 2002 to January 2003, Michael allowed a journalist unlimited access to his life. The documentary aired on ABC in early 2003.

I am Peter Pan in my heart.

Michael allowed the camera crew to tour Neverland Ranch. Michael said many strange things to the reporter.

Michael also said that his greatest inspiration came from kids.

Children don't lie to you. Children are pure and innocent and good.

On January 31, 2005, the *People v. Michael Jackson* began in Santa Maria, California. Michael was tried for child molestation. The trial was not related to the 1993 charges.

It's June 13, 2005. Mr. Jackson is not guilty.

The trial took a huge toll. Michael became dependent on prescription drugs. He lost a lot of weight.

I need to recharge.

Michael and the kids moved to Bahrain in the Persian Gulf.

Michael had money problems. He closed Neverland Ranch in 2006. He never returned.

CLOSED

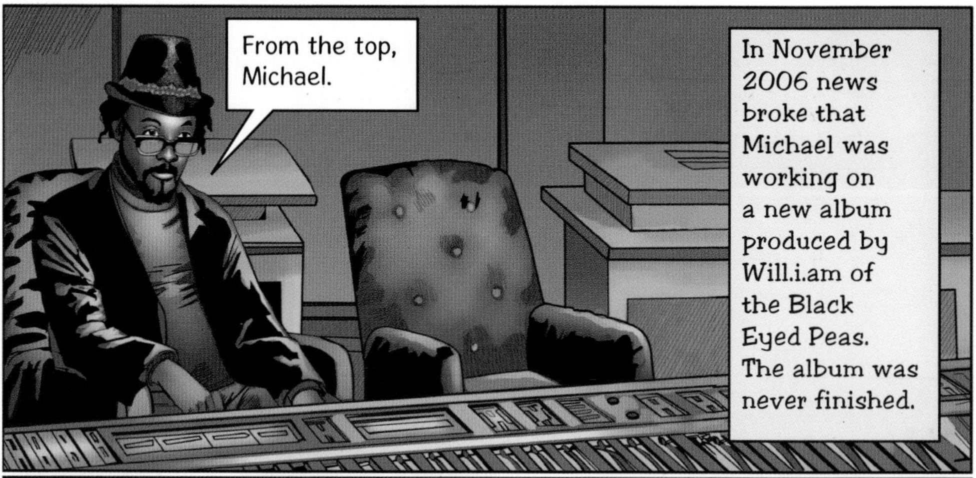
From the top, Michael.
In November 2006 news broke that Michael was working on a new album produced by Will.i.am of the Black Eyed Peas. The album was never finished.

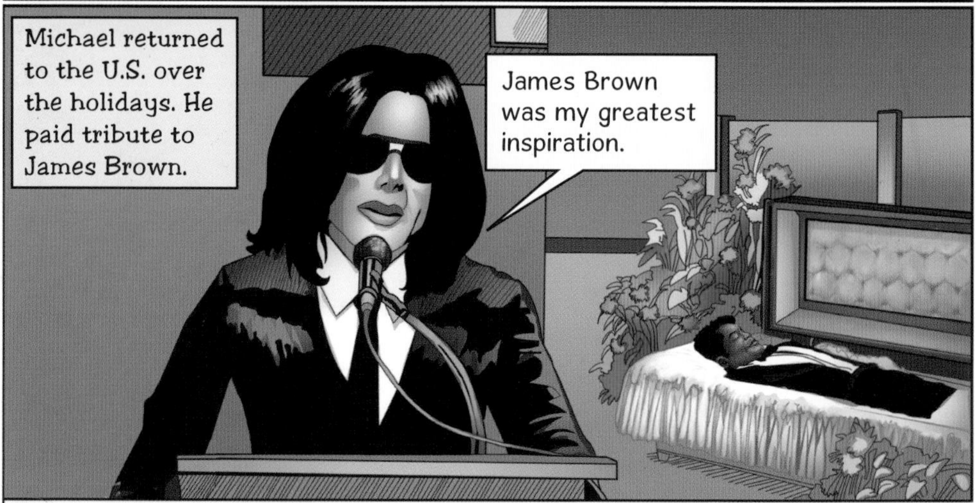
Michael returned to the U.S. over the holidays. He paid tribute to James Brown.
James Brown was my greatest inspiration.

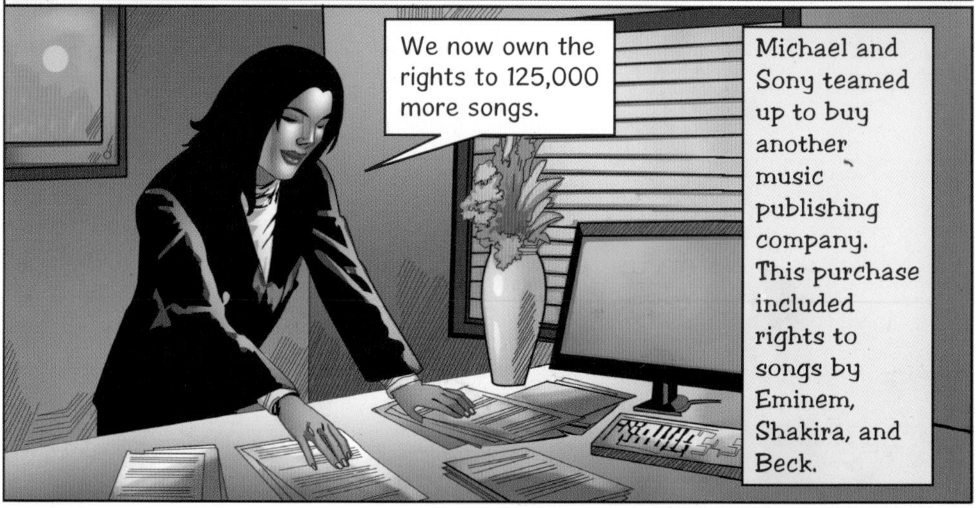
We now own the rights to 125,000 more songs.
Michael and Sony teamed up to buy another music publishing company. This purchase included rights to songs by Eminem, Shakira, and Beck.

In 2008 Jackson and Sony released *Thriller 25.* This album's release marked the 25th anniversary of the original *Thriller.* Five remixes featured artists like Akon and Kanye West.

Billie Jean is not my lover...

I said you wanna be startin' somethin', You got to be startin' somethin'...

You are spending a lot of money, Mr. Jackson.

Michael continued to have financial problems even with his music publishing investments.

In March 2009 Michael held a press conference in London. He announced a series of concerts in London's O$_2$ arena. The concerts were called "This Is It."

This is it. This is the final curtain call. See you in July.

After record-breaking ticket sales, the 10 planned concerts were expanded to 50. Over 1 million tickets were sold in less than two hours.

Did you score tickets to one of the concerts?

Michael rehearsed "This Is It" at Staples Center in Los Angeles. "This Is It" was scheduled to begin on July 13, 2009, and end in March of 2010.

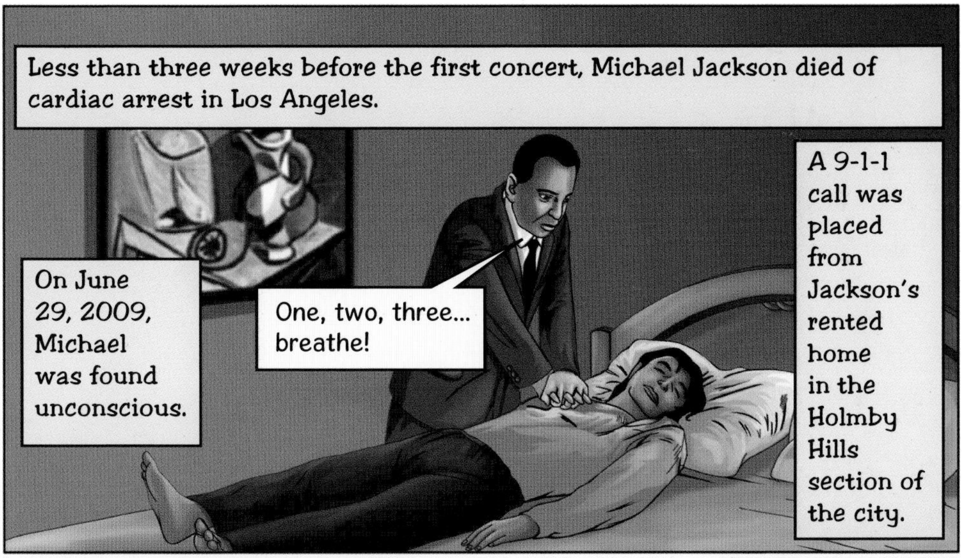
Less than three weeks before the first concert, Michael Jackson died of cardiac arrest in Los Angeles.
On June 29, 2009, Michael was found unconscious.
One, two, three... breathe!
A 9-1-1 call was placed from Jackson's rented home in the Holmby Hills section of the city.

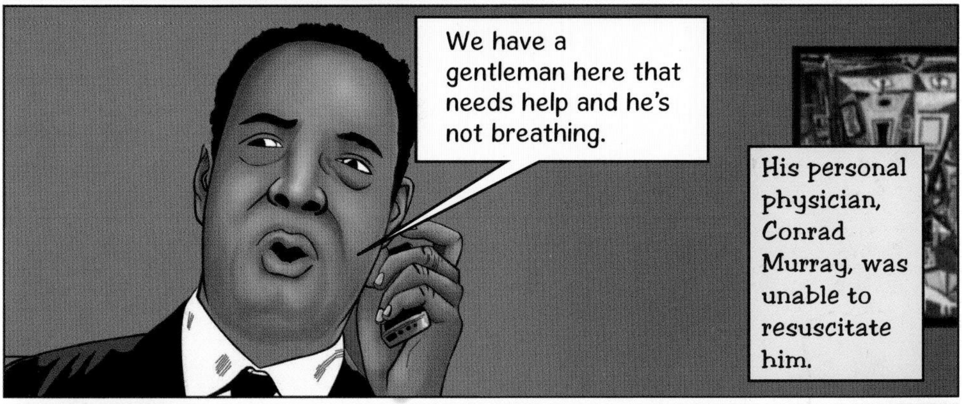
We have a gentleman here that needs help and he's not breathing.
His personal physician, Conrad Murray, was unable to resuscitate him.

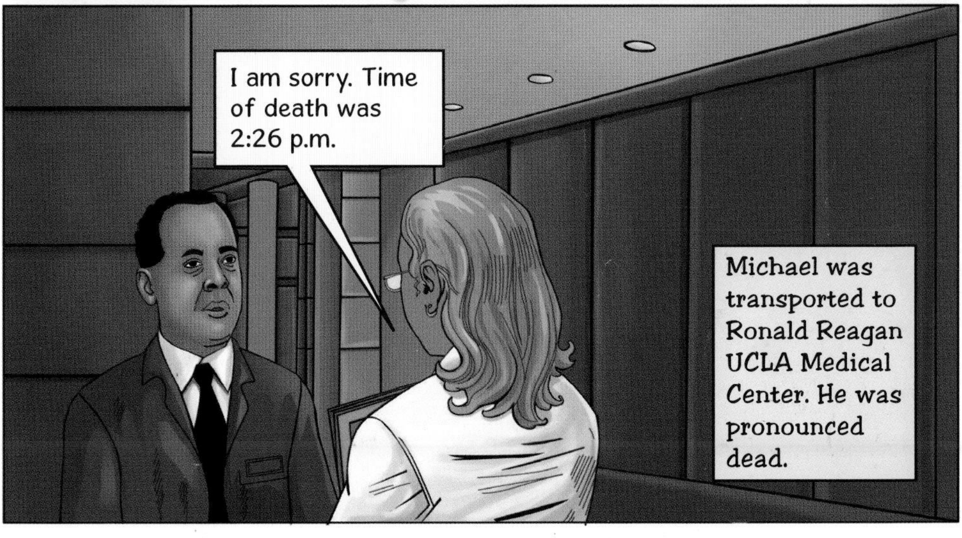
I am sorry. Time of death was 2:26 p.m.
Michael was transported to Ronald Reagan UCLA Medical Center. He was pronounced dead.

News of Michael's death swept the globe. Web sites crashed. Twitter and Wikipedia suffered outages. Grief gripped fans.

The world has lost a great artist.

This is such a massive loss on so many levels. Words fail me.

Lisa Marie

I can't stop crying over the sad news.

Madonna

Michael's memorial was held on July 7, 2009, in Los Angeles. Stevie Wonder, Lionel Richie, Mariah Carey, John Mayer, Jennifer Hudson, Usher, and many others sang in tribute to Michael. His daughter, Paris, told the crowd how much she loved her father.

Later that summer, the Los Angeles coroner decided to treat Jackson's death as a homicide.

SINGER · SONGWRITER · DANCER HUMANITARIAN · FATHER

During his extraordinary career, he sold an estimated 750 million records worldwide.

"I've been in the entertainment industry since I was six years old, and as Charles Dickens would say, 'It's been the best of times, the worst of times.' But I would not change my career..."

Michael was buried at Forest Lawn Memorial Park in Glendale, California.